Art & Activities for Kids

Make Cards!

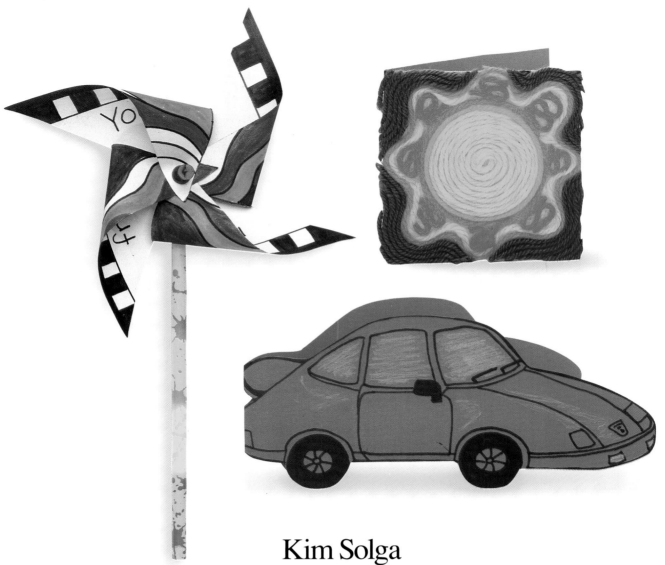

Kim Solga

NORTH
LIGHT
BOOKS

Cincinnati, Ohio

This hardcover edition of *Make Cards!* features a "self-jacket" that eliminates the need for a separate dust jacket. It provides sturdy protection for your book while it saves paper, trees and energy.

Other fine North Light Books are available from your local bookstore or direct from the publisher.

Published simultaneously in Canada by McGraw-Hill Ryerson Limited, 300 Water Street, Whitby, Ontario, L1N 9B6.

99 98 97 96 95   7 6 5 4 3

Library of Congress Cataloging-in-Publication Data

Solga, Kim.
    Make cards! / Kim Solga.—1st ed.
        p.   cm.—(Art & activities for kids)
    Summary: Instructions for creating greeting cards for all occasions.
    ISBN 0-89134-481-0 (hard)
    1. Greeting cards—Juvenile literature. [1. Greeting cards. 2. Handicraft.] I. Title. II. Series.
TT872.S67   1992
745.594'1—dc20   92-3431
                                                  CIP
                                                  AC

Edited by Julie Wesling Whaley
Design Direction by Clare Finney
Art Direction by Kristi Kane Cullen
Photography by Pamela Monfort
Very special thanks to Theresa Brockman, Jennifer Mayhall, Jeremy Moore, Kathy Savage-Hubbard, Niki Smith, Hallie Stiles, Suzanne Whitaker and Rachel Wolf.

Make Cards! features twenty-one projects that will fire the imaginations of boys and girls ages six to eleven, and will result in quality cards kids will be proud to give or send. By inviting children to design their own cards, *Make Cards!* encourages individual creativity. Young artists will love doing these activities even while they're learning the importance of fine craftsmanship. Also, they'll be learning composition and design, working with color and texture, and planning symmetry versus abstract design. They'll even learn traditional bookbinding techniques.

Make Cards! develops not only artistic skills, but also fine motor skills and problem-solving abilities. Kids will decide to whom to send a card and for what occasion, plan the design, and then collect objects and supplies to create with. They'll engineer pop-up cards and construct edible candy cards. They'll plan peek-a-boo window cards. (What will be the surprise inside?) They'll invent board games and dot-to-dot puzzles, jigsaw puzzles and mazes. They'll make cards that will become three-dimensional boxes and pinwheels. They'll also learn easy ways to make wrapping paper and envelopes.

Getting the Most Out of the Projects

In *Make Cards!* kids learn by doing. They'll gain confidence as they experiment in various craft mediums. Giving handmade cards satisfies a kid's need for recognition of his or her work, something that giving store-bought cards can't do. All the projects are kid-tested to ensure success.

While the projects provide clear step-by-step instructions and photographs, each is open-ended so kids may decide what kind of cards *they* want to make. Most of the cards are shown without words on them so that kids can fill in their own ideas. In the text next to the cards, we've suggested things the cards *could* say, just to get kids started. Most of the cards are easy to make in a short time. Others require more patience and even adult supervision. The symbols on pages 6 and 7 will help you recognize the more challenging activities.

Collecting Supplies

Pages 6 to 9 picture almost all the materials your child will need to make any of the cards in this book. You probably have 90 percent of them around your home already; the rest are inexpensive and easy to find at a supermarket, art supply store or craft store. Feel free to substitute! The projects offer flexibility to make it easy for you and your child to try as many activities as you wish.

A Word About Safety

The activities in this book were developed for the enjoyment of children. We've taken every precaution to ensure their safety and success. Please follow the directions and note where an adult's help is recommended. In fact, feel free to work alongside your young artists as often as you can. They will appreciate help in reading and learning new techniques, and will love the chance to talk and show off their creations. Children thrive on attention and praise, and art adventures are the perfect setting for both.

4

Be a Good Artist

Here are some art and school supplies you will need to make the cards in this book.

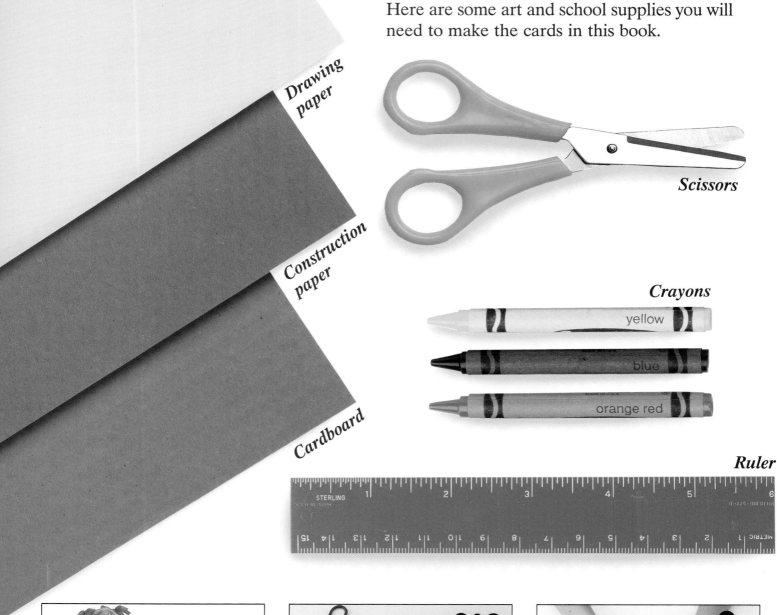

Drawing paper

Construction paper

Cardboard

Scissors

Crayons

yellow

blue

orange red

Ruler

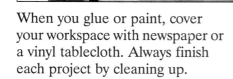

When you glue or paint, cover your workspace with newspaper or a vinyl tablecloth. Always finish each project by cleaning up.

The clock symbol means you must wait to let something dry before going on to the next step. It is very important not to rush ahead.

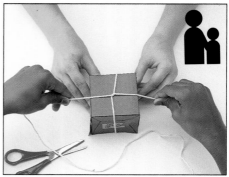

Follow the directions carefully for each project. Ask an adult for help if you need it.

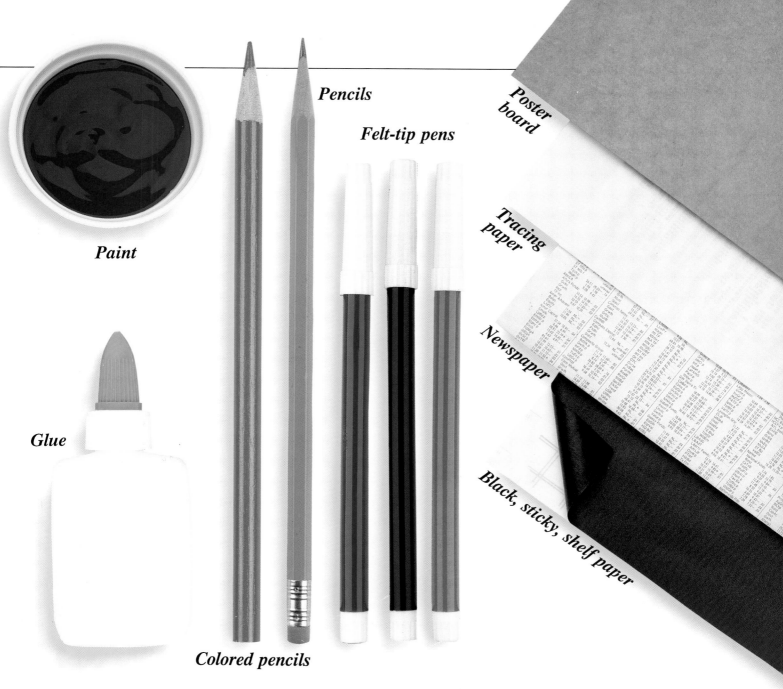

Paint

Pencils

Felt-tip pens

Poster board

Tracing paper

Newspaper

Black, sticky, shelf paper

Glue

Colored pencils

Get permission to use photographs on your cards. Or cut colorful pictures out of magazines and catalogs.

Don't put art materials in your mouth. If you're working with a younger child, don't let him put art materials in his mouth, either.

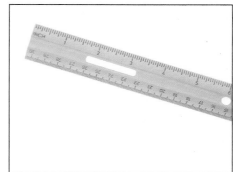

Use a ruler to measure. This symbol, ″, means inches (12″ means twelve inches). Cm means centimeters. (About 2½ cm equals 1″.)

Collecting Supplies

Here are some things you may use to make cards. You can probably find most of them around your home. If you have to buy some things, just remember that the cost of the supplies is part of the special gift — a card you made yourself!

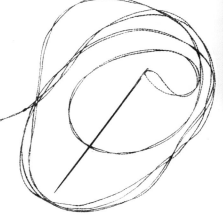

Needle and thread

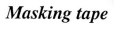

Graham crackers

Nail

Masking tape

Electrical tape

String

Fabric scraps

Straw

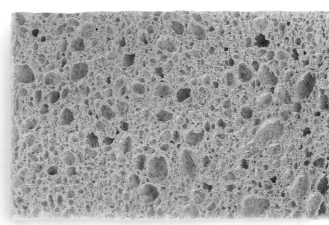

Sponge

Plastic wrap

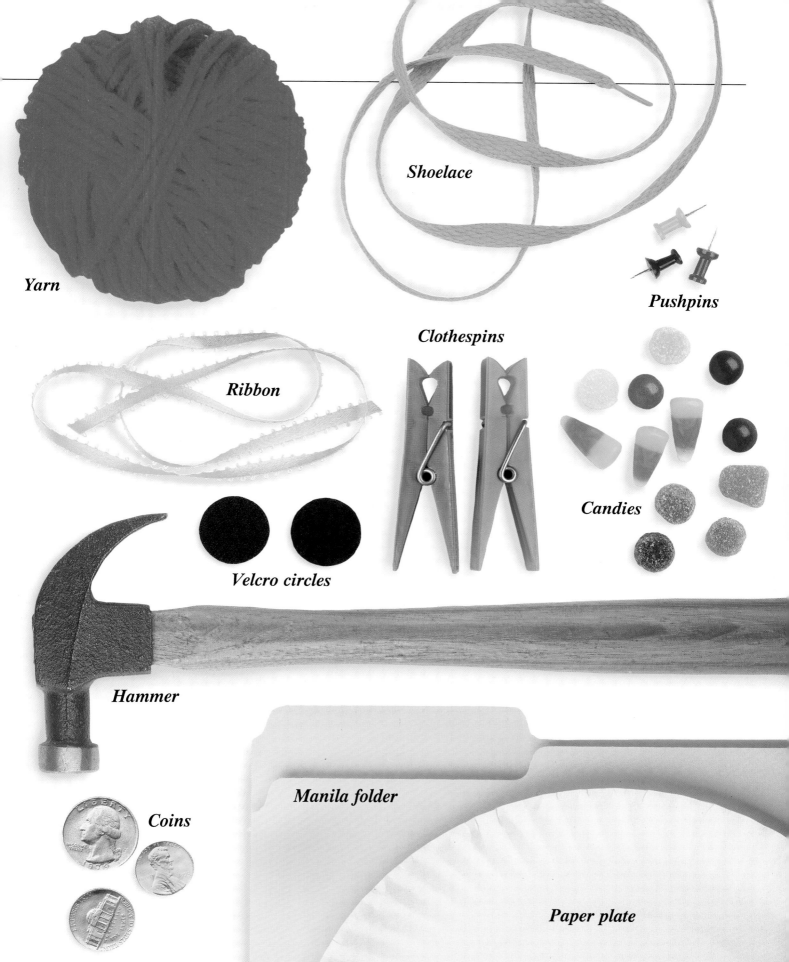

Yarn

Shoelace

Pushpins

Clothespins

Ribbon

Candies

Velcro circles

Hammer

Coins

Manila folder

Paper plate

9

Pull-Out Cards

There's more to these cards than meets the eye! They pull out and out and out to reveal a *long* message or picture.

Your card can pull out sideways or longways, whichever makes more sense for your picture. Glue a little tab on the back of the top panel for pulling.

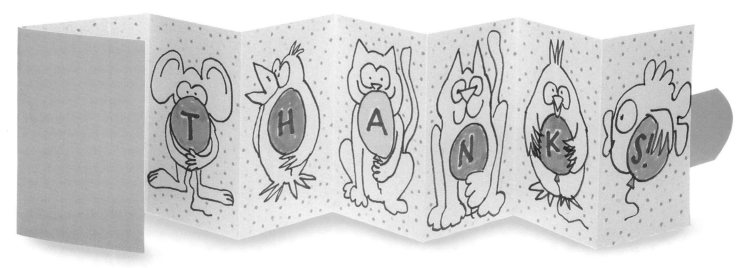

1 Make a cover for your card. Cut a piece of sturdy paper 6″ by 8″ (15 cm by 20 cm) and fold it in half. You can decorate the front of the cover if you wish.

2 Cut a strip of paper 6″ (15 cm) tall and 19″ (48 cm) long. Fold it like an accordion so each panel is about 3¾″ (9½ cm) wide.

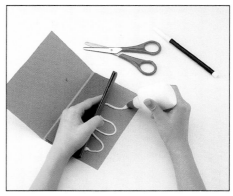

3 Glue the folded paper to the inside of the card cover. Make sure the top accordion fold is on the *inside* next to the fold of the cover.

Painted flowers growing tall make a
pretty Mother's Day card.

This card could say "Have a blast on
your anniversary."

11

Shape Cards

These cute cards come in any shape you want:
hearts, sports cars, pigs, pizza or letters.
You trim the edges to fit your design.

A car-shaped card could say
"Wishing you a *speedy* recovery."

Do you have a special friend you
could send a card to—in the shape of
his or her own name?

1 Fold a piece of paper in half to
make a card. The fold can be at
the top or the side of the card. Make
a drawing with one edge touching
the fold.

2 Color your picture with crayons,
paint or felt-tip pens. Draw a
smooth, solid line all around the
drawing if you wish.

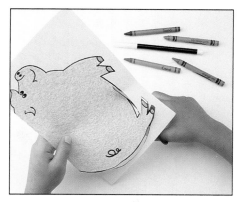

3 Cut along the outside line,
through both layers of paper.
Don't cut along the fold! Open your
shape, color the inside, and write a
message.

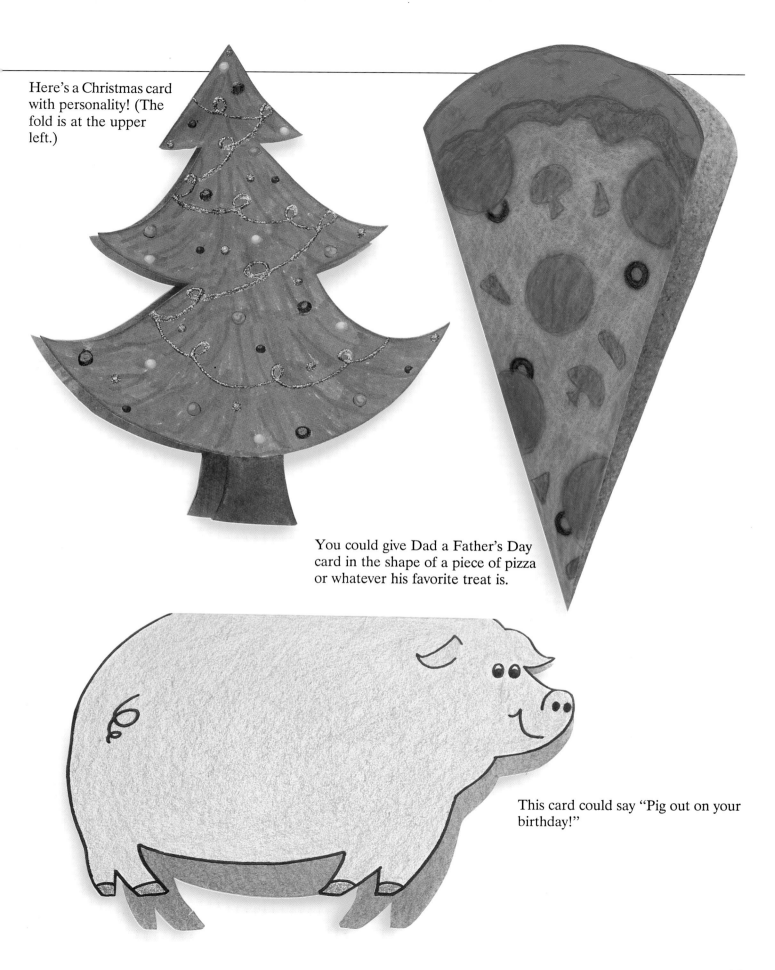

Here's a Christmas card with personality! (The fold is at the upper left.)

You could give Dad a Father's Day card in the shape of a piece of pizza or whatever his favorite treat is.

This card could say "Pig out on your birthday!"

13

Window Cards

These cards are sure to make someone smile. Cut a "window" in the front cover. Paste a photo or draw a picture on the inside. Only part of the picture shows through. When you open the card—surprise!

This house card could say "Congratulations on your new home."

A camera card.

This fence card could say "Have some good, clean fun this Grandparent's Day!"

A TV card could say "You're the star of the show!" Tape plastic wrap behind the window and it will look like a shiny TV screen.

Toy Cards

When is a card not just a card? When it's a toy! Send your friends something really special: a card they can play with. Send the pinwheel or snake flat, with directions for how to make them work.

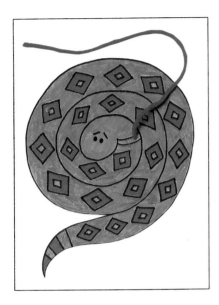

Silly Snake

Send the snake to someone as a flat card, shown above. Tell him or her to cut out the snake by cutting all the way up the spiral line and around the head.

When the snake is cut out, it will hang in a spiral as you can see to the right. Blow on it, and it will do a twisting dance!

Pinwheel

This pinwheel has two different sides. Before it's put together, it's just a flat square, shown at the top of the page. Send it to someone with a pushpin, a brand new pencil, and the directions (on the next page).

To the left you can see what the pinwheel looks like all folded up and ready to spin! Turn it around with your hands until it moves easily. Then blow on it for a really fast spin!

Pinwheel Card

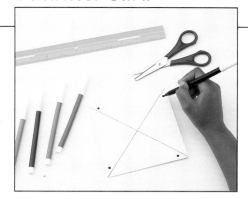

1 Cut a piece of heavy paper into a square that's 5″ (13 cm) on each side. Draw an "X." Make four dots, as shown.

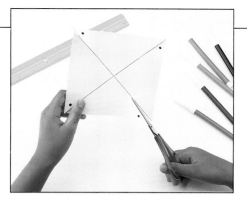

2 Cut each line 2½″ (6½ cm) in from the corners. *Don't* cut all the way to the middle! Poke a hole in the center with a nail or pushpin.

3 Decorate both sides of the pinwheel. This one says, "You're a nice friend" on one side, and has a colorful design on the back.

Pinwheel Directions

1 Here are directions to send with your card: Push the pushpin up through one of the corner dots. Bend the paper in so the pin is over the center hole.

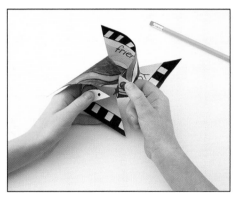

2 One by one, bend each paper corner under the pushpin and push up. Push all the other dots up onto the pin. Be careful not to poke your finger.

3 When all the corners are on the pushpin, push it through the center hole of the pinwheel. Poke it straight into the eraser of the pencil.

Silly Snake Card

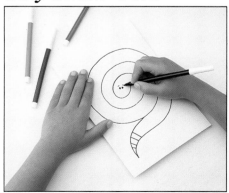

1 On the front of a folded card, draw a long snake all coiled up.

2 Decorate the snake with bold markings.

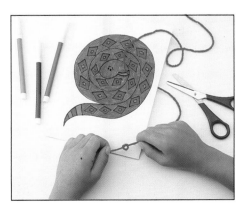

3 Color both sides of the snake. Poke a hole at the head of the snake. Tie on a long piece of yarn.

Game Cards

Game cards make good Get Well cards. On the front cover you could write "Hope you're feeling better soon. Here's a little something to cheer you."

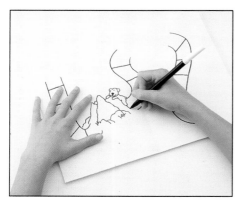

1 Fold a card out of strong paper 9″ by 12″ (size A4). On the inside, draw a path and divide it into spaces. Make barriers or shortcuts.

2 Draw a color in each space or write directions like, "Jump ahead 3 spaces." Draw pictures around the path.

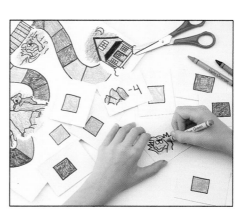

3 You can write instructions around the border of your game. Or make up cards to show players which space to move to.

START

GO BACK TO START

GO BACK 2

MISS ONE TURN

JUMP AHEAD 4

SWITCH WITH LEADER

MISS 2 TURNS

TAKE AN EXTRA TURN

GO BACK FOUR

GO BACK TO THE STAR

SKIP YOUR NEXT TURN

FINISH

YOU LAND ON AN ARROW, GO INTO THE SIDE

YOU LAND ON ANOTHER PLAYER, THEY GO

IF YOU LAND ON AN ARROW, GO INTO THE SIDE

BACK 4 SPACES. FIRST ONE TO THE FINISH WINS!

A finished board game.

You can buy dice and game pieces if you wish. Or, make cards to show where the players should move and use buttons or coins for game pieces.

Book Cards

Most cards are made up of just one piece of paper folded into two pages. But you can make a card that is a whole book of pages! The more pages you put in, the more it will look like a real book. Make a little joke book and write one of your favorite jokes or riddles on each page. Tie it with a shoelace for an extra laugh. Or make a book to fill with your special family photos.

A book of jokes and riddles.

A photo album. If you like how the stitches look, you don't *have* to cover them with tape.

1 Measure and cut two pieces of poster board for the book covers. Make lots of pages out of heavy paper or poster board. Cut them all the same size.

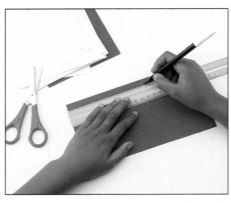

2 Use a ruler and make a line of dots along one edge of one of the covers. Make the marks 1″ (2½ cm) apart.

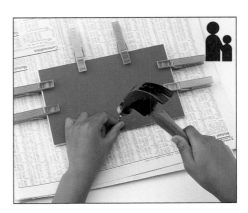

3 Stack the pages between the covers (put the marked cover on top). Hold it with clothespins. Set it on a stack of newspaper. Carefully nail a hole at each mark.

A picture book is the perfect card to say "Welcome, new baby." The cover looks like a building block. The inside pages are filled with big, colorful pictures for the baby to look at.

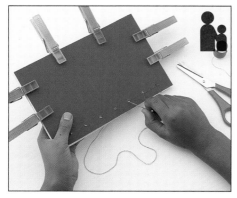

4 Cut a long piece of thread. Poke it through the hole of a needle. Bring the ends together and tie a knot. Make lots of stitches through the nail holes.

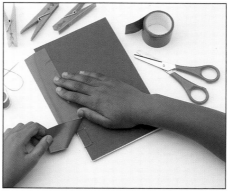

5 Wrap a strip of colored electrical tape or glue-covered paper around the edge of the book that is stitched.

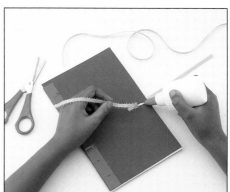

6 Glue a short piece of ribbon on the front and back covers. When the glue is dry, tie the book closed!

Book Cards

This house-shaped card is a family scrapbook. It is held together with *brads* (little, bendable metal clips). Each page has drawings and stuff collected from someone in the family.

▲ Here's the outside of the scrapbook.

Here's the inside of the scrapbook.

No-Bake Cookies   YUM!

Boil for one minute: 2 cups sugar
                     ½ cup milk
                     ½ cup margarine

Then add: 4 tablespoons cocoa powder
          1 cup chocolate chips
          1 teaspoon vanilla
          3 cups quick oats

Stir it up. Drop little balls of
dough onto waxed paper with
a teaspoon. Let them cool.
Then they are ready to eat!

Make an oven-shaped card! This one
is stapled instead of stitched. The
oven door opens to reveal all your
favorite recipes. A great card for
someone who loves to cook or bake.

Note Pad

A note pad "book card" is a very
useful gift!

Collage Cards

Piece by piece, bits of paper and scraps of cloth may not look like much. But put them all together and you can make beautiful *collage* cards. A collage is a picture made up of pieces of cut paper or other little things. Half the fun of collage cards is looking for stuff to make them with!

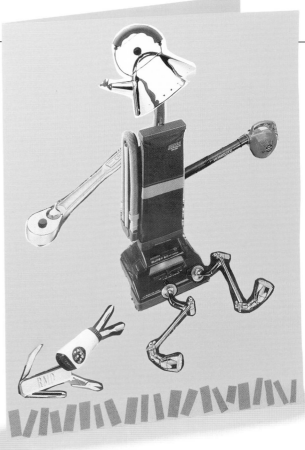

Paper collages are fun and easy to put together for any holiday or special occasion.

This robot looks like he's running away from a robot dog. He'd be a cheerful card for someone who is ill. The inside could say "Hope you're on your feet again soon!"

Paper collage. Cut pictures and letters out of old magazines. Arrange these pieces on the front of a folded card. Glue or tape them in place.

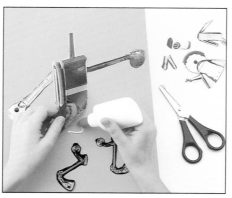

Radical robots. Look through magazines and catalogs for pictures of machines and metal things. Carefully cut them out and glue them together to make robots.

Country quilts. Cut scraps of cloth into little squares. Glue them on the front of a folded card. Draw stitches around each square.

Quilt collage cards can say "I'm glad we're friends," or any message you want to send. Cutting with *pinking shears* makes the cloth edges zigzagged.

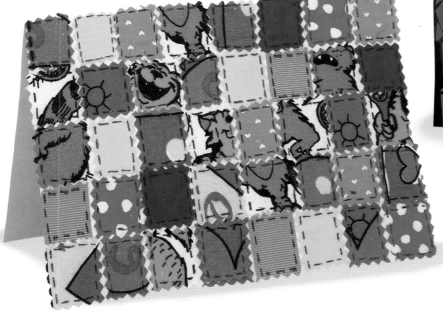

This rainbow really looks like a *mosaic* made of colored tiles. Glue or tape your finished mosaic onto the front of a folded card.

Tile Mosaic Card

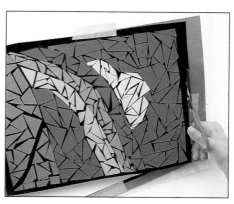

1 Cut a piece of black, sticky, shelf paper. Place it sticky-side-up on a piece of cardboard. Hold the edges down with masking tape.

2 Cut little shapes out of colored paper. Stick them on the black paper to make an abstract design or a picture. Leave a little black between the shapes.

3 Cut a piece of clear, sticky, shelf paper to fit over your mosaic. Carefully put it sticky-side-down. Smooth it and trim the edges. Cut the masking tape off, too.

Collage Cards

A candy collage makes a sweet treat for any special day.

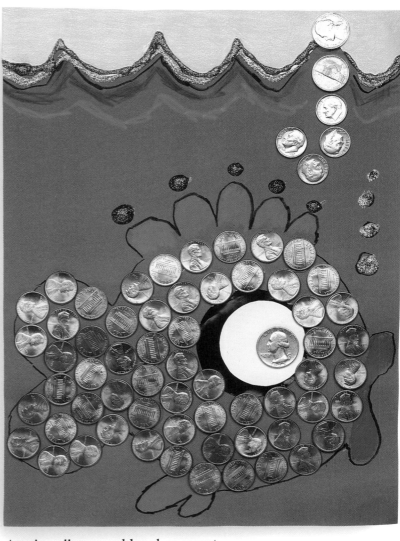

A coin collage would make a great "Good luck" card.

Candy Card

1 You will need small candies like candy corn and chocolate bits. Arrange them on a graham cracker so they make a picture.

2 Make frosting "glue" by stirring a teaspoon of milk or water into ¼ cup of powdered sugar.

3 One at a time, lift the candies off the cracker. Dip just the bottoms into frosting. Set them back in place. Let it dry overnight.

Straw collage card

A collage of lace, flowers, hearts and cupids makes a beautiful valentine.

Straw Card

1 Cut a cardboard rectangle. Paint it black—acrylic paint is best. Let the paint dry.

2 Cut the straw into strips. Glue these onto the black board to create a picture. When you're done, let the glue dry completely.

3 Brush acrylic varnish over the finished picture. When it's dry, glue it onto the front of a folded card a little bigger than the board.

Print Cards

Dip a cookie cutter in paint and stamp it to make a print. Or, cut wild shapes out of foam or sponges to print with. It's so much fun, you'll want to make lots of these easy print cards. You can also make wrapping paper to match!

Print cards are fun and easy to make just to say "Thinking of you," "I miss you," or "Please write."

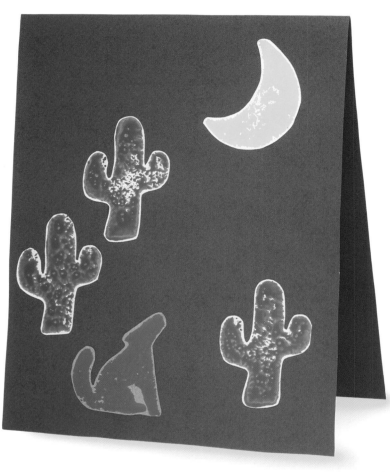

A heart-shaped friendship card.

Sponge Stamps

1 You can buy little sponge shapes to make prints with. Or, cut your own simple shapes out of sponges or foam.

2 Spread a thin layer of tempera paint on a plate. Press a sponge shape into the paint. Then stamp it onto paper to make a print.

3 Make lots of prints. Pick the best ones, cut them out, and glue them onto your card.

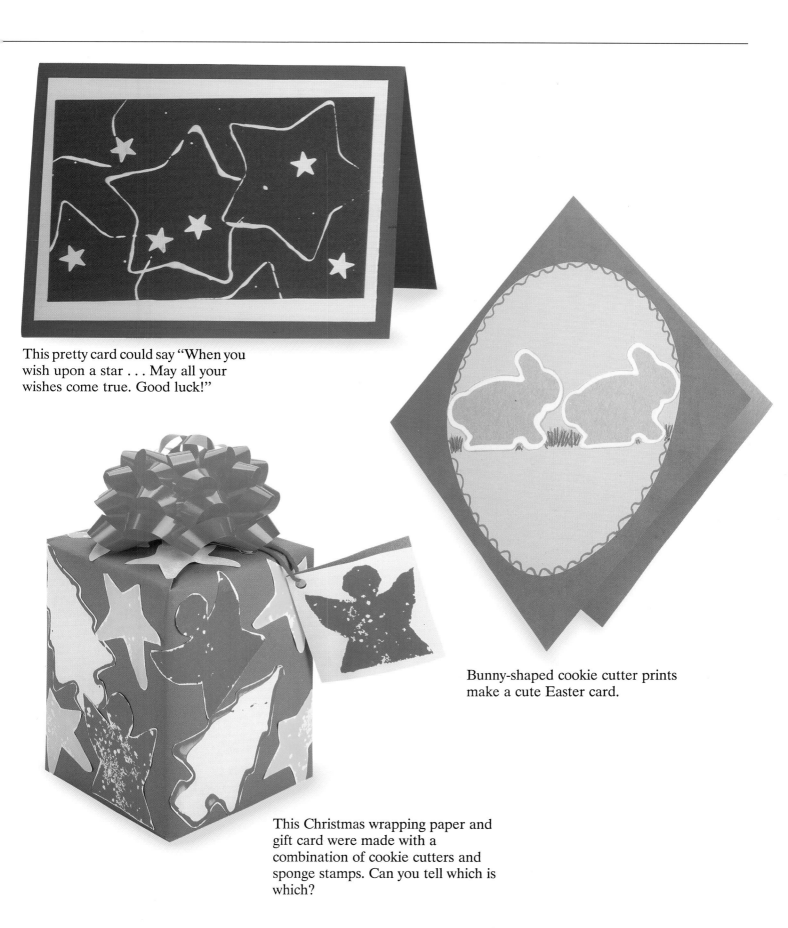

This pretty card could say "When you wish upon a star . . . May all your wishes come true. Good luck!"

Bunny-shaped cookie cutter prints make a cute Easter card.

This Christmas wrapping paper and gift card were made with a combination of cookie cutters and sponge stamps. Can you tell which is which?

Trickster Cards

Here are some tricky cards your friends and relatives will love to open. After you try these four ideas, make up your own special trickster cards!

A briefcase card makes a perfect birthday card for a hardworking dad or mom.

Briefcase Card

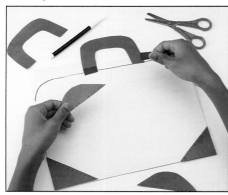

1 Draw a briefcase on a manila folder with the bottom edge on the fold. Color your drawing or use cut paper to make your card look like a real briefcase.

2 Cut out the briefcase shape. Decorate the inside of the card to look like the inside of a briefcase. Put velcro circles in the top corners to hold it closed.

3 Cut strips of paper to make pockets and glue them inside the briefcase. Make little paper pens, a note pad and a calculator.

This box is made of two layers of paper glued together. A manila folder makes it strong. Brown paper makes it look like a real mailing package.

Box Card

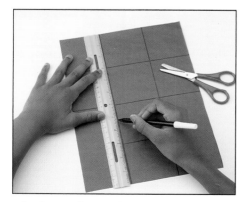

1 On a piece of sturdy paper 9″ by 12″ (size A4), draw a 3″ (7 cm) square. Then draw five more squares the same size to make a cross shape.

2 Cut out the cross shape. Fold at each line you drew to make six squares. Open it up and decorate the outside to look like a package.

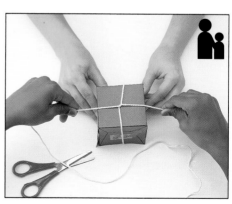

3 Write your message on the inside. Fold the box and tie it closed with a piece of string. (It's easier to tie if someone holds it closed for you.)

Trickster Cards

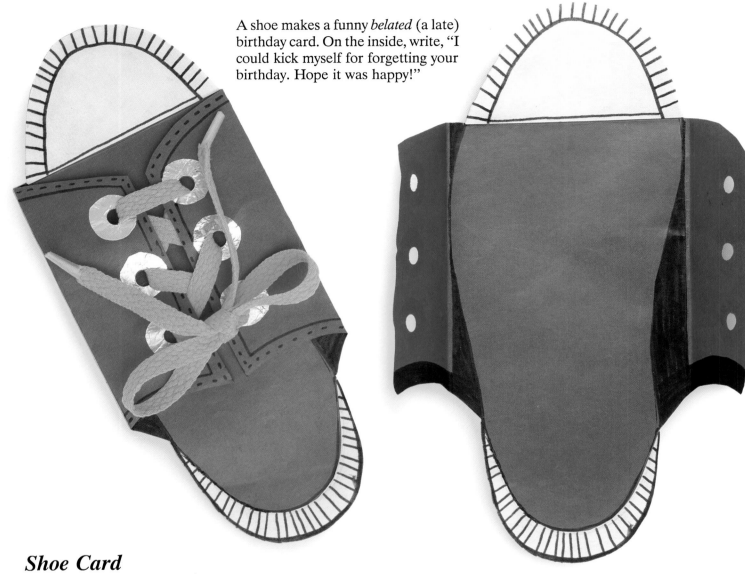

A shoe makes a funny *belated* (a late) birthday card. On the inside, write, "I could kick myself for forgetting your birthday. Hope it was happy!"

Shoe Card

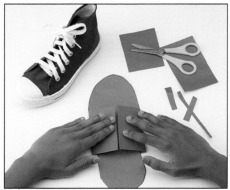

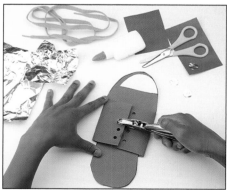

1 Put a shoe in the middle of a big piece of sturdy paper and trace around it. Use the shoe as a guide when you color your card.

2 Draw flaps on both sides of the shoe. Cut out the shoe and flaps as one big piece. Make the flaps big at first, then fold them in and trim them until they meet in the middle.

3 Make holes in the flaps for the laces. A hole punch works best. Write a message under the flaps and decorate the shoe with colored paper and foil.

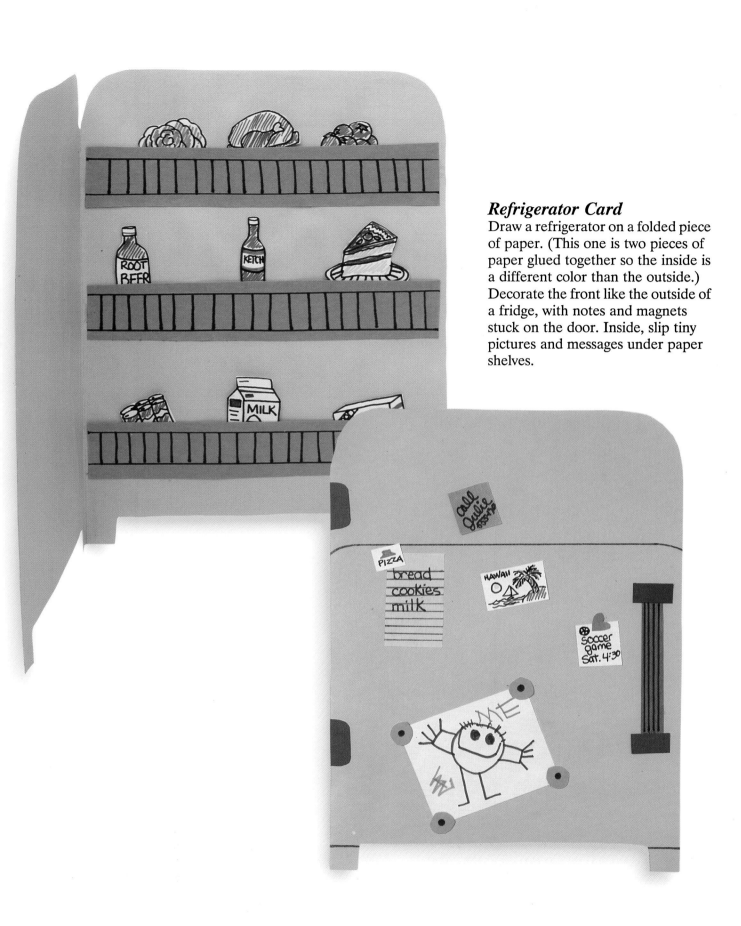

Refrigerator Card

Draw a refrigerator on a folded piece of paper. (This one is two pieces of paper glued together so the inside is a different color than the outside.) Decorate the front like the outside of a fridge, with notes and magnets stuck on the door. Inside, slip tiny pictures and messages under paper shelves.

Yarn Cards

These cards are soft, fuzzy and fun to touch. You make the designs with pieces of brightly colored yarn.

Finished Flower Card

Gift Card

Flower Card

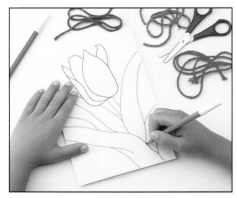

1 Draw a simple picture on the front of a folded card. Cut long pieces of yarn in the colors you want for your picture.

2 Squeeze a thin line of white glue along the lines you drew. Gently lay the yarn along the glue lines. Push the yarn down into the glue as you go.

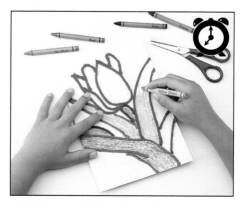

3 Cover all the lines in your drawing with yarn. Let the glue dry. Then color the paper behind your yarn drawing with felt pens or crayons.

Good Luck Card
This rainbow was painted with watercolor paints. Then yarn was added between the stripes of color.

Note Card
This duck was made like the flower card, but yarn was used instead of crayons to color in all the shapes.

Hi, Grandma! Hi, Grandpa!

Use a hole punch or scissors to make holes around the front cover of a card. Then weave yarn in and out to make a frame for a cute photograph. It's easier to weave if you wrap tape around the tip of the yarn.

We've Moved

Cut a scrap of checkered material. Stitch X's in the checks to make a picture. Glue the picture onto the front of a card!

Great Ball o' Yarn

Collect little toys and candies. Tie them onto a *long* piece of yarn as you wind it into a big ball. Keep wrapping until all the toys and candies are hidden inside the ball of yarn. When your friend unwinds the ball of yarn, she'll discover one surprise after another!

Personalized Birthday Card

Cover the front of a card with sticky shelf paper that looks like wood. Use string or twine to write a name. The "I" in this card was dotted with a metal "spur" for a real Western look.

Wedding Card

Cut a small piece of mesh from a bag of apples or oranges. Cut a hole into the front of a card. Tape the mesh on the *inside* of the front of the card, covering the hole. Weave yarn into the mesh and decorate the front of the card.

Pop-Up Cards

These fancy cards really stand up to the occasion! Open them—and a silly face, birthday cake, spaceship, or vase of flowers pops to life. You build the 3-D designs with special folds and paper hinges.

Here's the inside of the face pop-up card—going bonkers!

Here's the cover of a face pop-up card.

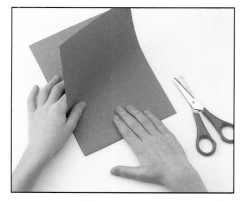

1 Cut and fold a sturdy piece of paper to make a card cover.

2 Cut out the pieces you need for your picture. On this person, the shirt and head are flat against the inside of the card, so they are glued down first.

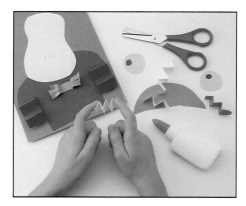

3 Make paper "springs." Cut three thin strips of paper. Fold them into zigzags. On this person, the bow tie and arms were folded into zigzags, too.

This festive cake pops up for a very Happy Birthday card.

This card could say "Your gift was out of this world! Thank you!"

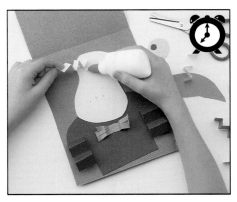

4 Glue one end of each spring onto the card where you want something to pop up. Let the glue dry before going on.

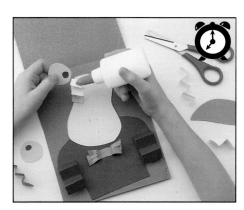

5 Glue the other end of each spring to the back of a pop-up piece. Let the glue dry. When you close the card, gently fold the springs closed.

6 Add decorations. This person has swirls for nostrils, a zigzag tongue, hands, buttons and ribbons.

Pop-Up Cards

Here's the finished flower vase card. Be careful when you close this card—don't smash the flowers! Send it to someone to say "Thank you," "Get well," "Congratulations," or for any occasion when you might send flowers.

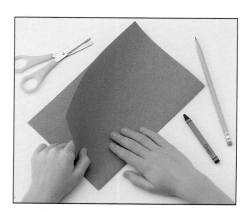

1 Here's another way to make a pop-up card. Start by making a sturdy paper cover.

2 For a flower vase card, cut flowers and stems out of colorful construction paper.

3 Cut a paper vase. It should be a little smaller than half the size of your card. Fold it in half. Fold each edge back to make two flaps.

You can make a "sideways" pop-up card. The "V"-shaped fold makes a park bench for kids and animals to sit on! This card could say "Happy Birthday" or "You are special."

4 Open the card cover. Hold the vase over the center fold. Hold it so the "V" shape stands up a little. Mark one of the flap edges.

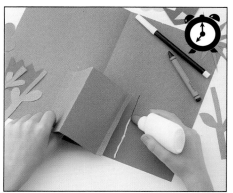

5 Spread glue along the line and set the flap down in place. Glue the other flap to the other side of the cover. Let it dry.

6 Glue some of the flowers to the card cover. Glue some to the inside of the vase so they pop up. Add sequins and cut paper shapes.

Puzzle Cards

Give your friends and family something to think about with these mysterious puzzle cards. Make a jigsaw puzzle or hidden message card — they'll have to solve the puzzle to get your message. Or design a dot-to-dot puzzle or a maze just for fun. You can make them easy to do or hard to do — it's up to you!

Here's how your jigsaw puzzle card will look when it's cut into pieces.

Here's another puzzle card before it's cut apart. You could send it to someone just to celebrate the first day of summer (June 21).

Jigsaw Puzzle

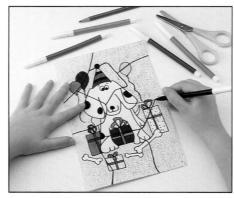

1 Draw a picture on a piece of heavy paper. Color your picture with crayons, colored pencils or felt-tip pens. Write a message in big letters on the back.

2 Divide your picture into puzzle pieces. Draw twisty lines in black. Make all the pieces about the same size — and not too small.

3 Cut the pieces apart and put them in an envelope. The person who gets this card will have to put the puzzle together to read the message on the back.

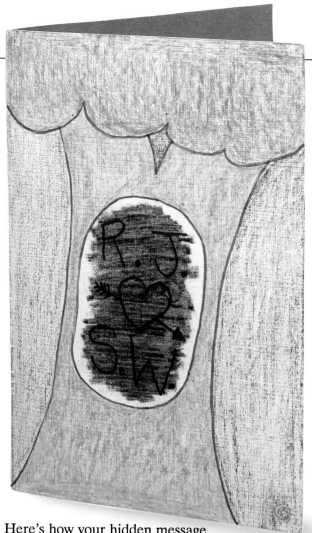

Here's how your hidden message card will look when the person scratches off the black. Use the entire inside of the card to write a love letter!

Another way to send a secret message is to write on white paper with a white crayon. The special instructions would say "To read this card, paint it with watercolors!"

Hidden Message

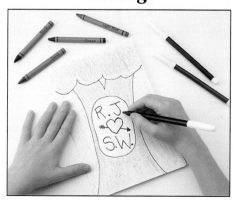

1 Write a message on a card, by itself or inside a drawing. This card is made to look like initials carved into a tree.

2 Color over the whole message with black crayon. Make it dark so the message doesn't show through the black.

3 With this card, send special instructions that say: "To read this card, use a coin to scratch off the black crayon."

Puzzle Cards

Dot-to-Dot

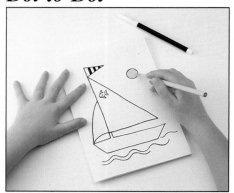  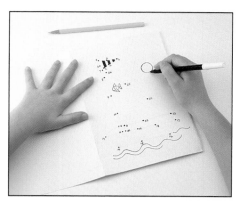

1 Fold a piece of paper in half. Draw a simple picture on one half. Fold another piece and lay it on top. This top paper will be the card.

2 Draw dots along the lines of the main thing in your drawing. Make a dot wherever the lines change direction. Number the dots.

3 Draw the details that are not part of the dot-to-dot drawing. Make a colorful border around the card, if you wish.

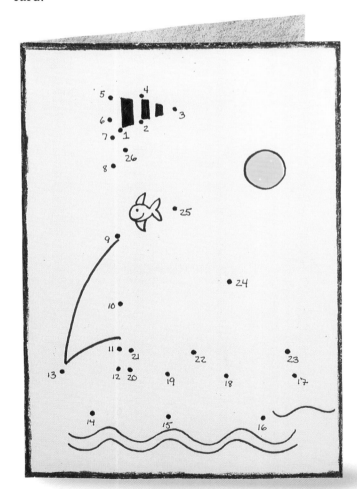

Here's how your finished dot-to-dot card will look when your friend gets it.

Here's how your puzzle will look after your friend has filled it in! Inside, it could say "Have a great vacation!"

Maze

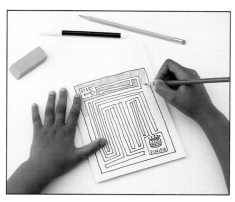

1 Draw a simple path. Then start to make dead-end paths (shown here in red). Erase the main path where the dead-ends begin.

2 Add more dead-end paths until you can hardly tell what the real path is! The more dead-ends you add, the harder it will be to solve.

3 Go over all the lines of your puzzle with a black felt-tip pen. Be careful to cover the lines completely. Color in the background.

Here's how a maze can become an invitation. On a photocopy machine, you can make lots of copies on colored paper. Use crayons to add extra color. On the inside, write:

Who: _____ (your name)
What: <u>A Birthday Party!</u>
Where: _____ (your address)
When: _____ (the date and time of the party)
RSVP: _____ (your phone number —this means people should call and tell you if they can come). Make envelopes to send them in. See pages 46-47 for envelope instructions.

Envelopes

Make beautiful envelopes to fit all of your special cards. Use writing paper, colored construction paper, or the inside of a paper grocery bag! If you are going to mail your envelope, use shelf paper (from a supermarket). It's light and sturdy, and it won't get hurt if it gets wet.

▲ This looks like an envelope. It's really a letter folded in thirds and held together with a sticker.

◀ Finished basic envelope from the back.

Basic Envelope

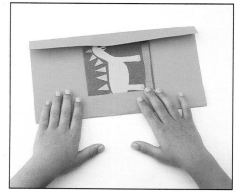

1 Lay your card in the middle of a big piece of paper. Fold the two sides of the paper in over the card.

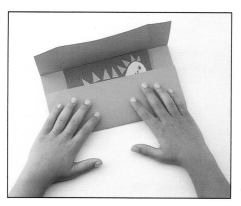

2 Fold the bottom edge up over the card and the top edge down. The card should fit perfectly inside the folds.

3 Open the folds and cut out the corner rectangles.

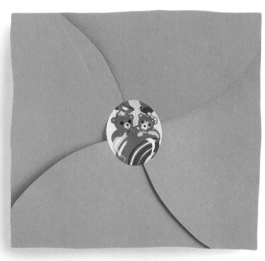

Make a fancy envelope for a square card. Cut four flaps like flower petals. Fold them over the card one at a time. Hold them together with a sticker.

4 Fold slanted flaps on the top and bottom parts of the envelope.

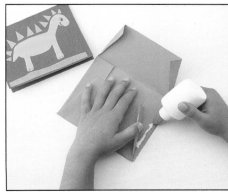

5 Fold the sides of the envelope in. Fold the bottom up and glue the flaps to the sides of the envelope.

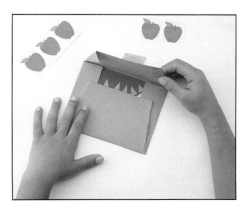

6 Slip the card inside and fold the top of the envelope down over it. Glue it down or hold it with a sticker.

47